The Milk of Hathor

Happy Milky Days!

♡ Heather Dundee

a.k.a the Goddess of moo—

This book is dedicated to Fiona who showed me that
love doesn't divide, it expands
(and oh! so many other ways that I am limitless...)
And to Kevin for being unlimited and expansive, too.

Printed and Distributed by Lulu.com
Or direct from the artist at
www.thecowgoddess.com

ISBN 978-1-4303-0740-2

The Milk of Hathor

The Breastfeeding Comics
2002-2006

by Heather Cushman-Dowdee

Breastmilk
2002-2006

AND NOW...
A SHORT, NOT QUITE TRUE (NOR THOROUGH)
HISTORY
OOPS! SHOULD SAY HERSTORY!
OF
BREASTFEEDING
ACCORDING TO HATHOR THE COWGODDESS
(PRONE TO RAMBLING IN NON-LINEAR FASHION, BECAUSE LACTATING AND THE DEMANDS OF SMALL CHILDREN MAKE IT SO THAT MAGNIFICENT MAMAS CAN'T THINK STRAIGHT.)
YET, STILL PRESENTED AS A TIMELINE...

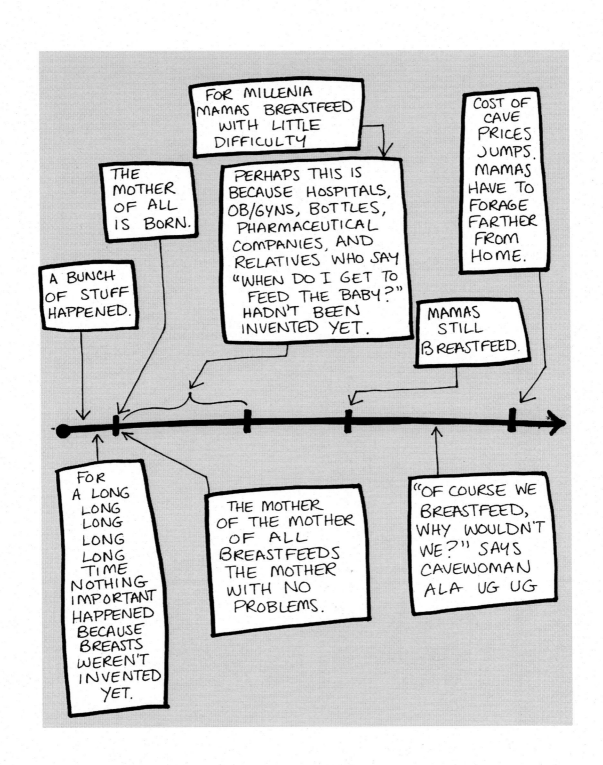

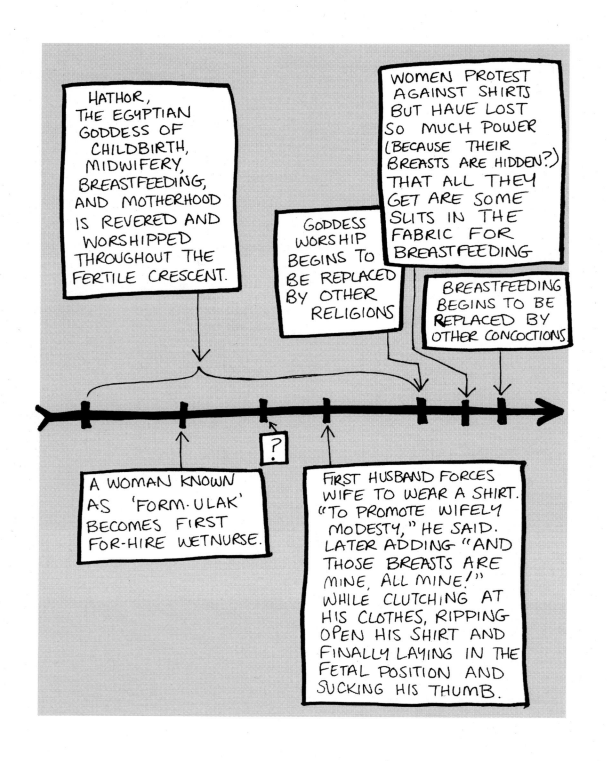

HATHOR, THE EGYPTIAN GODDESS OF CHILDBIRTH, MIDWIFERY, BREASTFEEDING, AND MOTHERHOOD IS REVERED AND WORSHIPPED THROUGHOUT THE FERTILE CRESCENT.

WOMEN PROTEST AGAINST SHIRTS BUT HAVE LOST SO MUCH POWER (BECAUSE THEIR BREASTS ARE HIDDEN?) THAT ALL THEY GET ARE SOME SLITS IN THE FABRIC FOR BREASTFEEDING

GODDESS WORSHIP BEGINS TO BE REPLACED BY OTHER RELIGIONS

BREASTFEEDING BEGINS TO BE REPLACED BY OTHER CONCOCTIONS.

?

A WOMAN KNOWN AS 'FORM·ULAK' BECOMES FIRST FOR-HIRE WETNURSE.

FIRST HUSBAND FORCES WIFE TO WEAR A SHIRT. "TO PROMOTE WIFELY MODESTY," HE SAID. LATER ADDING "AND THOSE BREASTS ARE MINE, ALL MINE!" WHILE CLUTCHING AT HIS CLOTHES, RIPPING OPEN HIS SHIRT AND FINALLY LAYING IN THE FETAL POSITION AND SUCKING HIS THUMB.

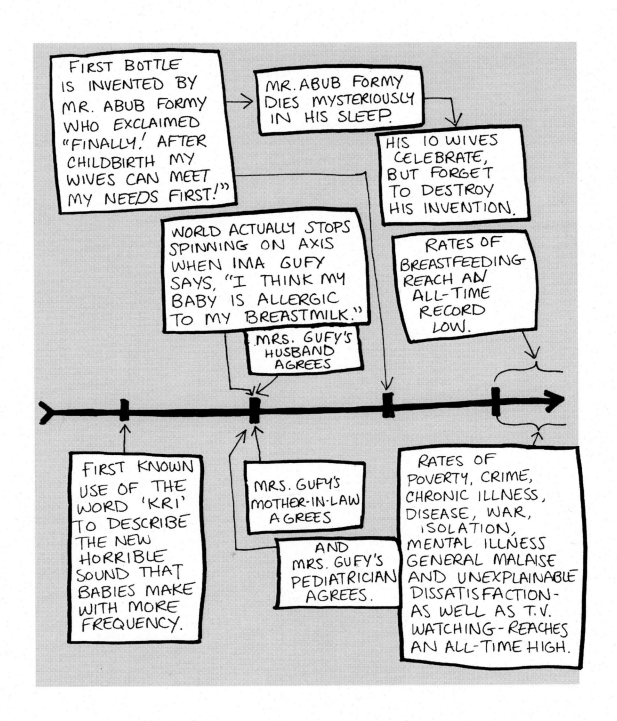

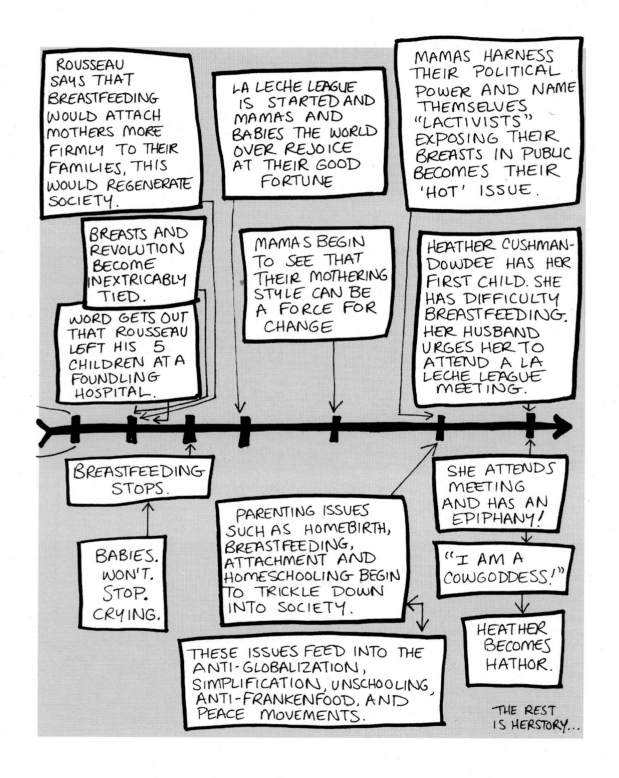

Cowgoddess Culture

So, let's just jump right into the dream…in a Cowgoddess Culture, homebirths become commonplace, medical interventions into birth decline and women gain much needed self-confidence in their health and the health of their children. So much so that the entire medical community is reorganized into a system in which patients of both sexes have an equal voice with their doctors about their paths to wellness.

Consultation with a health professional would of course be paid for by barter, with no family paying more than they are capable of giving. (As a matter of fact the insurance companies would have to be the first to go). And in a Cowgoddess culture those condescending doctors would no longer be able to think of themselves as god-like. Their false hierarchy would collapse.

Breastfeeding would become the acceptable norm, and a bottle would be looked on in sympathy. Breasts would be everywhere, happy children nursing contentedly on every surface of the earth. There would be quiet as the sound of crying babies slowly left the planet. If a baby were found motherless, Cowgoddesses would collaborate to make sure it is fed. The world population begins to decline because of natural child spacing through breastfeeding. Pharmaceutical companies hit hard, pack their bags and stop selling their snake oil. Finally health is not about profit.

Babies would sleep with their parents. Parenting would no longer be a billion-dollar industry. Cowgoddesses wouldn't need anything beyond their breast and a sling. Houses would become smaller and more intimate. Families would find that even after working and playing together all day, they still like each other enough to spend time in the same rooms. Land use would decline dramatically, and the urge to keep up with the Jones's would disappear.

Does this mean that women become housewives and mere breeding machines? No! Women have always combined work and childcare; presently however, work has gotten so much more interesting and takes her out into the public sphere. But, why not babies too? The Cowgoddesses surge into the work force with babies tied onto their backs.

Sure, work slows down for breastfeeding, playtime and napping breaks, but this benefits even the men on the workforce. Everyone gets more work done, is more rested and more satisfied with their working environment. And with all the job places becoming family friendly and lifestyles becoming simplified, people begin to choose work that is creative and fulfilling instead of just for the paycheck.

When Cowgoddesses run the show, environmental concerns (there are pesticides in breastmilk! For goddess' sake!) take the forefront. The safety and availability of food, air and water become Issue Number One on their agenda. Pollution ceases because we say so.

Then one day a Cowgoddess remarks, "All this breastfeeding makes me hungry and thirsty". Using this as a battle cry, the divine bovines rush the gates of the food stores, the food is unlocked and freely handed out, and the entire economic culture is restructured to include cooperative farming and living. Consumer culture becomes nothing but a nasty memory.

Once babies have had a taste of the real world from the sling on their parents' back, they are no longer content to grow up within the confines of the concentration camp-like schools. Children freely roam the cities and towns, accessing mentors, information and books and following any path of learning they may find interesting. Cowgoddesses and their partners restructure city planning so those children can travel unhindered. Mass transit becomes the norm, cars become antiquated ideas, and roads become avenues for walking and biking.

As this generation of Cowgoddesses' offspring reaches maturity there is a renaissance of creativity, invention and ideas the likes of which the world has never known.

23

Why I Wear This Old Nursing Bra....

In my long and illustrious breastfeeding career I have experienced:

Cracked nipples,

Itching nipples,

Inverted nipples and

Mastitis not once but 5 times!

Once on my birthday.

Also itchy breasts.

As well as and probably pertaining to…

Poor positioning,

Poor latch,

High palates,

Colic

And these must be related to the

Excessive milk production

Which resulted in

A wee bit of post-partum depression and

Exuberant block nursing

And elimination diets,

Which proved inconclusive…

Also,

Been bitten

And both of my older girls weaned when I was pregnant.

I cried. A lot.

Yet still, I remain (possibly) the world's biggest proponent of breastfeeding.

Because when it works it's oh so good.

When nursing works for me I believe it is directly related to my lucky nursing bras.

I kid you not!

It is an underwire bra, which holds my breasts up.

And it has top closure which means I don't ever have to close it and it still works.

I buy it too many sizes too big so that when it is closed it creates a wrinkle of fabric, which never touches skin.

It is from Target and they no longer sell that particular style.

I have two left.

They are grey and forlorn. Oh, oh, lucky bras....

HATHOR the COWGODDESS

IN THE DISTANCE WE WITNESS AN 8 MONTH OLD SUCKLING FROM HER HUMAN MOTHER, A PEACEFUL SCENE OF TRANQUILITY AND LOVE...

HUMAN? HUMAN!? I AM A COWGODDESS IN ACTION!

YET UP CLOSE YOU'LL SEE SKIN PULLED, PUSHED PINCHED AND KNEADED BEYOND WHAT IT SEEMS HUMANLY POSSIBLE TO ENDURE.

SEE? THAT'S WHAT I'M SAYING! THAT'S ONE OF MY MANY DIVINE QUALITIES!

SQUISHY! GWISHY! WIGGWY! LOVE!

*HATHOR IS A THIRD TIME MAMA, PLEASE DO NOT TRY THIS AT HOME...

HATHOR the COWGODDESS

HATHOR the COWGODDESS

53

The Politics of Breastfeeding
2002-2006

THIS YEAR, I WILL TRY TO BE A MOTHERING ROLE-MODEL BY ATTENTIVELY NURTURING MY CHILD WHENEVER AND WHEREVER I AM NEEDED.

MANIFESTO ISSUE #2: BREASTFEED ON DEMAND

HATHOR the COWGODDESS

continued on next page…

©2003 HEATHER CUSHMAN-DOWDEE

The Time Waster Movement

Okay. Let's take stock of the situation. In August 2003, Real Simple(tons) Magazine called us breastfeeding mamas time wasters. They called our babies wastes of time and dismissed their health as unimportant. They mocked our miracles. So now what?

Stay at home breastfeeding mamas have (for quite a while) tried to gain legitimacy in this dog-eat-dog, materialistic, capitalism rules, consumer-driven economy. We have declared that all mothers are working mothers, we have threatened that we would like to be paid for our labor, we have accounted for our hours, and demanded ourselves salaries. In short, we have been trying very hard to be legitimate. To be an honest-to-god part of the labor force. To no avail. No matter how hard we try we can't make this look like hard work. Sure there are the endless errands, the tight money management, and the constant needs of 4 foot and under tyrants. We all know we work like dogs, and that our work is never done. (Look at us standing at the sink doing the last load of dishes at 10:00 PM. It's the third load of the day; we're practically saints.)

Yeah we work hard. But there's the love, the bliss, the happy giggles of our children, and the hours spent outside, the playing, that always interfere and cause the legitimate paid work force (men and women alike) to consider us on a permanent vacation. Yeah right. But, hey, maybe…yeah right. YEAH RIGHT! Like a feminist encountering the word bitch (derogatory) in a glossy rag and embracing it, and taking it on as a badge. Or an African American that uses the N-word as a friendly aside. Perhaps it's time for us to embrace the insults that are being hurled at us. Find our strength in our attributes and use it, to our advantage.

I have long considered myself a feminist, an environmentalist, an anti-globalization-ist(?), a peace-nik, a neo-hip(ster)py. A lactivist. An artist. A mother. It's the first time I've been called a Time Waster. But hey, that can fit too. Every one of these titles puts me in direct opposition to the powers that be. I'm one of many in the opposition, but still hopelessly outnumbered, at times truly powerless. Which is, I think, why we mamas seek legitimacy, we think it is the only way to enter the Big Conversation about the economy, the government, and the culture. We think it's the only way we'll be listened to.

But I've changed my mind. The powers that be can have their Big Conversation. It's time for us to start our own, on our front stoops, in our back yards, in the parks. It's how we will win the revolution of thought, by having so much fun, wasting so much time, and embracing such acts of idleness that the work force can't help but be jealous. They'll have to join us, and with massive numbers, we will gain that legitimacy, but on our own terms. Think of it, can you imagine a mother who really wouldn't want (deep down) to spend more time with her kids? Parents who wouldn't rather spend more time playing? People who wouldn't rather spend more time outdoors? What if every time workers looked out a window they saw us playing tag in the grass? Or every trip to the grocery store saw mamas juggling fruits to giggling children? The disdain would vanish, and everyone would begin to want a piece of the action.

And if the labor force awakens to say "Hey, I want to waste my time with my children too." What would happen? A massive shift in priorities. Quite probably painful at first, but worth it in the long run. Look around at the stay at home mamas you know, not rich monetarily but kind of blissed-out rich in their spirit. They've got different priorities. Imagine that for the whole culture. Everyone not rich, just blissed-out rich in his or her spirit. Wow. Love and giggles, miles of picnic blankets, frontyard gardens, bike paths everywhere, small farms, and work cooperatives. Solar panels and giant windows on the world. Everyone doing work they love and loving whom they are with. That's the Evolution Revolution I dream about, and who would have thought I'd get there by wasting my time?

Want to join the Time Waster movement? There aren't any rules but one. Just run outside and play, breastfeed your babies in public, make your presence known, erupt into inappropriate laughter, dance in crowds, and hug your children with joy. Come on mamas, let the revolution begin!

69

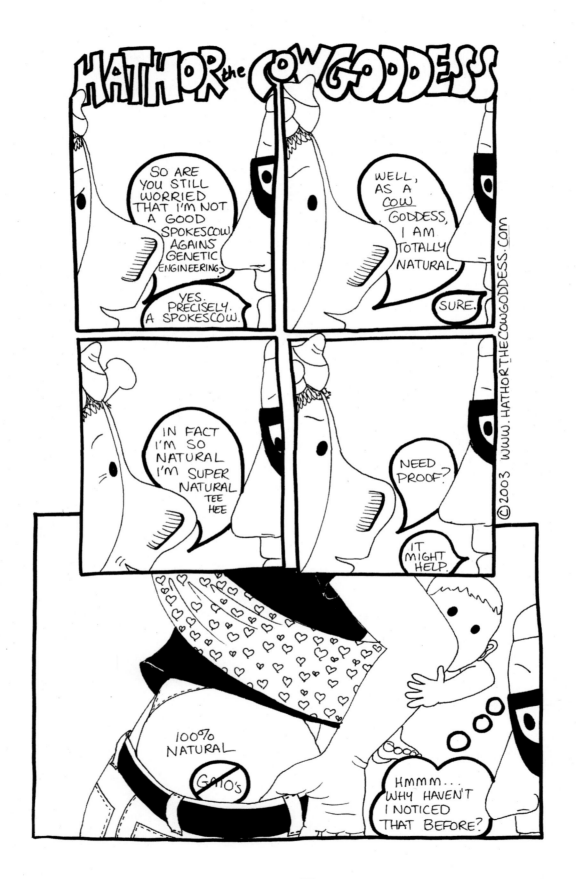

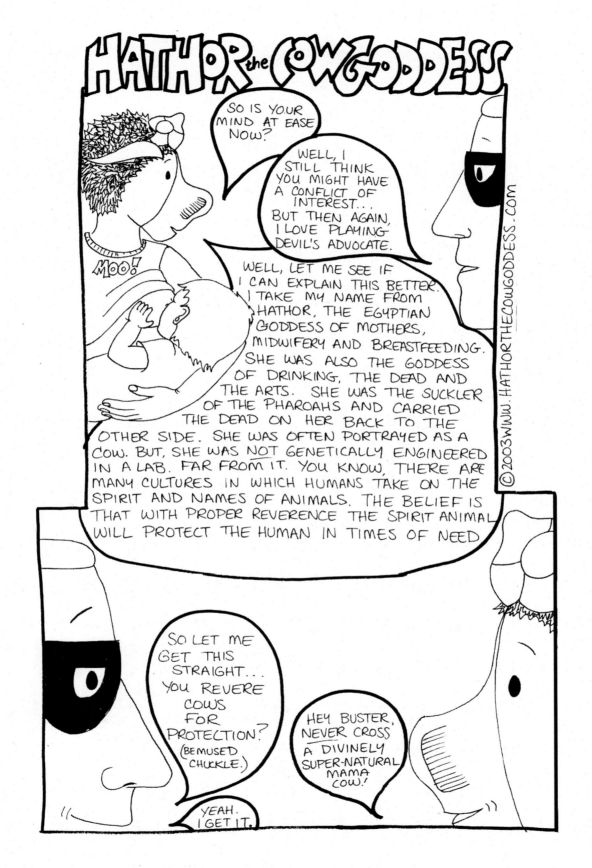

Attending La Leche League Meetings <u>Is</u> Political Action

1. **La Leche League-ers believe that mothering through breastfeeding is the most natural and effective way of understanding and satisfying the needs of the baby.** Everyone who has heard the never-ending cries of an unsatisfied baby knows that a happy, satisfied baby makes a happy, empowered mommy. An empowered mommy can protest, meet, boycott, collect, blockade, pontificate and agitate. Just try to stop her.

2. **La Leche League-ers believe that mother and baby need to be together early and often to establish a satisfying relationship and an adequate milk supply.** This early bonding gives a baby its first taste of breastmilk, but also its first taste of intense love, security, dependence and peace. Perhaps it gives a mommy her first taste of love, security, dependence and peace, too. And that's got to be good for everyone.

3. **La Leche League-ers believe that in the early years the baby has an intense need to be with his mother, which is as basic as his need for food.** Oh, how empowering to be needed so; radicalizing to be needed so. And the babies, oh how liberating! Where mommy goes, so goes the baby. Babies see the world and the world has to slow down, adapt, accommodate, and accede to the babies.

4. **La Leche League-ers believe that breastmilk is the superior infant food.** Down with the mega-capitalist, super-global formula corporations and their peddling of chemical processes in a can. Down with the pharmaceutical mega-monopolies' over-medicalization of our lives. Down with the profit-driven hospitals, and pandering physicians who pay lip service to breastfeeding while accepting loans, grants and

82

donations from entities responsible for the starvation deaths of millions of children. Up with the mommies, up with their delicious, whole, bountiful, breastmilk!

5. **La Leche League-ers believe that for the healthy, full term baby, breastmilk is the only food necessary until baby shows signs of needing solids, about the middle of the first year after birth.** This allows baby and mother to develop their exclusive, mutually dependent, all-encompassing relationship for at least half a year. Maybe more. That should teach the old hurry-up, faster, faster, keep up or get-out-of-the-way world. SLOW DOWN. Slow down, for the babies.

6. **La Leche League-ers believe that ideally, the breastfeeding relationship will continue until the baby outgrows the need.** Okay, we've come a long way. In this day and age, many have gotten used to the idea of breasts feeding babies. But toddlers? Pre-schoolers? Even school age children? This makes our culture, which reveres the breast as an object of sexuality, and confers ownership of said mammary glands to the one whose gaze rests upon them, VERY uncomfortable. Incredibly uncomfortable. Obscenely uncomfortable. Yaaaay! So show the world that you own your breasts, by publicly breastfeeding those kids.

7. **La Leche League-ers believe that alert, active participation by the mother in childbirth is a help in getting breastfeeding off to a good start.** A lot of women in our culture believe that having a choice of pharmaceuticals (to take the edge off of labor) shows feminist progress. But here's the truth. Obstetricians and hospital personnel will want to use sonograms to estimate un-estimable due dates. Will want to hook you up to continuous fetal-heart rate monitors, which will make it impossible for you to move around freely. Will want to stand around staring at those gadgets instead of supporting

and acknowledging you. They will urge induction at the expense of your own unknowable internal clock and that induction will make your contractions so strong so unbearable that you will beg for an epidural. They will push epidurals and other forms of pain medication on you because without them you are like a wild animal, powerful, but totally out of their control. And, lastly any of these interventions can rapidly lead to a cesarean section. You don't want a cesarean section. These people are not your friends. Choose a midwife. Birth in a freestanding birthcenter or better yet at home. Through natural childbirth you will be empowered, radicalized and yes, a feminist.

8. **La Leche League-ers believe that breastfeeding is enhanced and the nursing couple sustained by the loving support, help, and companionship of the baby's father. A father's unique relationship with his baby is an important element in the child's development from early infancy.** The men in our midst have a lot to gain and nothing to lose in becoming deeply bonded with their children; when they rise to the occasion it makes us all stronger. Sure, it's true, no mommy and not one baby need an authoritarian, patriarchal, abusive, unbending father figure. They need a daddy. (Or if that's impossible mommy needs a supportive partner of some kind.) And everyone needs a community (that celebrates cowgoddessness!) to raise a child well.

9. **La Leche League-ers believe that good nutrition means eating a well-balanced and varied diet of foods in as close to their natural state as possible.** Just say no to the yuck, yuck, frankenfood, the pesticide dripping produce, the genetically altered grains, the fat-infested fried grossness. You won't put it into your baby, not after the wonderfulness that is breastfeeding, and I'm willing to bet that you won't put it in

yourself either. Embrace whole foods and home-cooked, slow-food-ism. Eat your fruits and veggies!

10. **La Leche League-ers believe that from infancy on, children need loving guidance, which reflects acceptance of their capabilities and sensitivity to their feelings.**
Aaaaaaah, fewer NOs, and more YESes. Less yelling and screaming, more hugs and peacefulness reigns. Still the battlefield. And from your house the stillness spreads.

This list of 10 beliefs lays the cornerstones for just about every political movement from the last century. Feminism, Peace, Anti-Globalization. Go to a meeting, you'll see. Talk to a mommy there, she probably gave birth at home, she probably shares a family bed, she may be breastfeeding more than one child, she might be vegetarian, she may not vaccinate, there's a possibility she homeschools. She's got a baby in a sling and she's a radical. She believes in the sweet, sweet breastmilk and consequentially her beliefs feed the babies and build the next generations. Think of it this way, Mommies aren't just breastfeeding babies; they're starting an Evolution Revolution. And what could be more political than that?

HATHOR the COWGODDESS

So, is America ready?

Can breasts, babies, and some arbitrary ideas of decency co-exist in public?

I mean, 2004 was the year of Janet Jackson's 'accidental' exposure. And breastfeeding incidents in Burger King, Starbucks, and J.C. Penney's. I even heard about a mama who was escorted out of a government building by security guards... for nursing! Mamas, we've got a lot of work to do.

Thankfully we're used to hard work.

So here's to the new year! May the babies be nourished and us mamas have courage!

www.HATHORTHECOWGODDESS.com

© 2005 HEATHER CUSHMAN-DOWDEE

HATHOR the COWGODDESS

YAY! THE UNITED NATIONS AND WORLD HEALTH ORGANIZATION ARE PASSING A RESOLUTION IN SUPPORT OF BREASTFEEDING

IMAGINE! FIRST, THEY ACKNOWLEDGE ITS WORTH AND BENEFITS...

THEN THEY WILL ACCOMODATE US! SEE OUR WORK AS VALUABLE! MAYBE WE COULD GET BENEFITS AND SOCIAL SECURITY!

AND FINALLY... WE COULD INCLUDE BREASTMILK IN THE GROSS NATIONAL PRODUCT. MOTHERS WILL GAIN ECONOMIC POWER AND SURELY POLITICAL POWER WILL FOLLOW!

AND WITH POWER WE CAN DEMAND TRUE COST ACCOUNTING. AN ECONOMY THAT REWARDS PEOPLE WHO PUT GOOD INTO IT... POLLUTERS AND PILLAGERS AND

WAR MONGERS WILL LOSE THEIR GRIP ON OUR CULTURE. SOON... MOTHERS WILL RULE THE WORLD!

A U.S. REPRESENTATIVE WANTS TO PRESSURE W.H.O. **NOT** TO PASS THE PRO-BREASTFEEDING RESOLUTION, BECAUSE IT'S "JEOPARDIZING 100 YEARS OF PROGRESS BY WOMEN."

SO CLOSE! YET STILL SO FAR.

WWW.THECOWGODDESS.COM

© 2005 HEATHER CUSHMAN-DOWDEE

Nursing In Public
2002-2006

HATHOR the COWGODDESS

www.THECOWGODDESS.com

PRESS RELEASE

CITY OF CHANDLER, ARIZONA
WHERE VALUES MAKE THE DIFFERENCE.

HEAR YE! HEAR YE! ON THIS DAY FORWARD THERE IS A NEW RULE, PASSED WITHOUT OBJECTIONS BY THIS CITY'S ESTEEMED COUNCIL.

NO BABY SHALL EAT ON CITY PROPERTY.

ALL BABIES WILL HERE TO FORWARD EAT IN TOTAL SECRECY, MUST REMAIN HIDDEN FOR THE DURATION OF THEIR MEAL, OR IF FOUND, SUFFER THE CONSEQUENCES. ANY ADULT WHO SEES A BABY IN THE ACT OF EATING WILL COMPLAIN TO A CITY EMPLOYEE WHO WILL, IN TURN NOTIFY A SUPERVISOR. SAID SUPERVISOR WILL DETERMINE WHETHER THE BABY IS "UNREASONABLY DISTURBING OTHER MEMBERS OF THE PUBLIC". BABIES WHO REFUSE TO EAT IN SECRECY WILL BE ASKED TO LEAVE THE BUILDING OR GROUNDS. FAILURE TO LEAVE WILL RESULT IN CRIMINAL TRESPASSING CHARGES.

126

HATHOR the COWGODDESS

IN CONJUNCTION WITH THE AMERICAN ACADEMY OF PEDIATRICS' RECENTLY CREATED 'GUIDELINES', I'VE COME UP WITH MY OWN NEW GUIDELINE...

FROM NOW ON, ALL ADULTS WHO WERE PREVIOUSLY BABIES ARE NOT ALLOWED TO RESTRICT, LIMIT OR OTHERWISE HINDER THE FEEDING OF BABIES.
        PERIOD.

I MEAN COME ON!

IF YOU'VE MADE IT TO ADULTHOOD THEN YOU WERE PROBABLY FED WHEN YOU WERE A BABY. AS WERE YOUR PARENTS AND GRANDPARENTS AND SO ON...

IT'S JUST UNCOOL TO TURN AROUND NOW ALL GROWN UP, WITH A FULL TUMMY AND SAY 'BABIES SHOULDN'T EAT IN PUBLIC' OR 'BABIES ONLY NEED TO EAT EVERY THREE HOURS' OR 'BABIES SHOULD BE WEANED WHEN THEY REACH A CERTAIN AGE" YEAH. THAT'S EASY FOR YOU TO SAY, YOU EAT WHEREVER YOU WANT WHEN YOU'RE HUNGRY. SO FROM NOW ON GIVE YOUR FULL TUMMY A PAT AND SMILE OVER AT THE BREASTFEEDING BABY AND SAY "BON APPETIT!" IT'S ONLY FAIR.

BOOBI!-Action League
Somewhere in the USA

Dear Every Newspaper Editor,

Would you like to increase your readership through controversy? Create notoriety for your commentaries? Instant celebrity for a columnist? Would you like to use the word breast over and over again to titillate (see #2 below) your audience? Then I urge you to write an editorial condemning the act of breastfeeding in public and help us stop this cultural scourge before it spreads. Here's a quick template to help you, help us.

1. Pick a writer that has some relationship with breastfeeding. Are they a parent who did it once? Were they once a baby? Someone who has seen breastfeeding and was grossed out by it? Mention the writer's connection first thing, so that your readers will know that they have an expert opinion.

2. The writer should mention that she didn't want to write this article, but had to get it 'off her chest' (for fun, scatter breast puns throughout the article!) The writer should also admit that she knows she will recieve hatemail from 'hysterical' women. This immediately puts offended mothers on the defensive and now your writer seems funny and kind of nice.

3. Now let the insults fly! Other columnists have called breastfeeding 'obscene' and 'disgusting'. Get creative with your own derisive descriptions. Some columnists have gotten rave reviews for calling mothers 'militants' and 'breast-nazis', see if you can come up with even better names! And of course, compare breastfeeding to 'urinating' and 'defecating', popular culture loves scatalogical comparisons.

4. Finally, the writer should demand that breastfeeding mothers and babies be completely segregated from public view. (And you thought the fun of minority segregation was a thing of the past!)

That's all you have to do! And don't worry about any repurcussions or boycotts...babies have no political power and breastfeeding mothers don't have any power either.
Heck, they can barely hold down a job! So go ahead, bash away and everyone wins (except for mothers and babies, but who cares? Breastfeeding is gross!)

Sincerely,

Breastfeeding is Obscene and i'm Outraged By It!-Action League

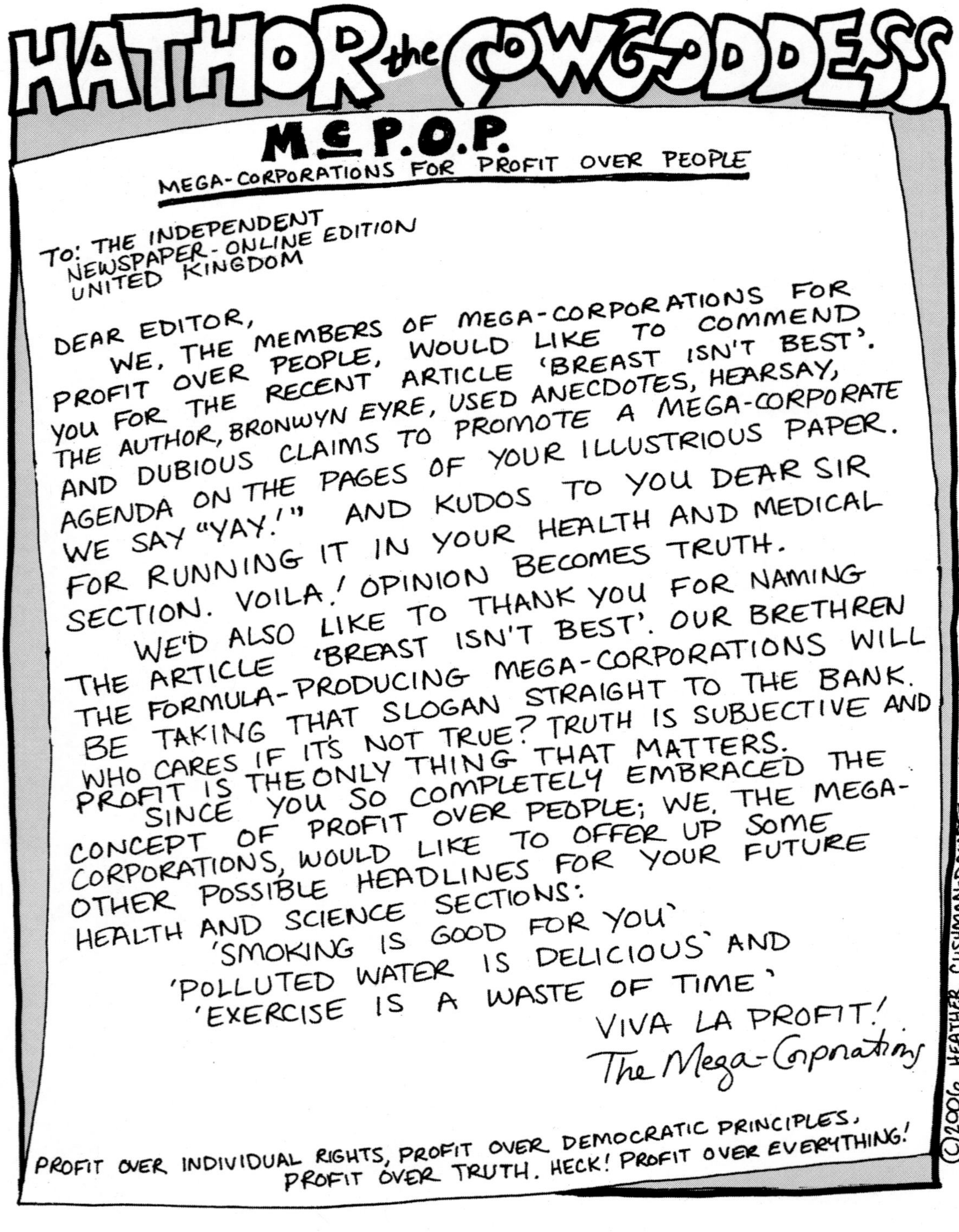

HATHOR the COWGODDESS

M©P.O.P.
MEGA-CORPORATIONS FOR PROFIT OVER PEOPLE

TO: THE INDEPENDENT
NEWSPAPER-ONLINE EDITION
UNITED KINGDOM

DEAR EDITOR,
WE, THE MEMBERS OF MEGA-CORPORATIONS FOR PROFIT OVER PEOPLE, WOULD LIKE TO COMMEND YOU FOR THE RECENT ARTICLE 'BREAST ISN'T BEST'. THE AUTHOR, BRONWYN EYRE, USED ANECDOTES, HEARSAY, AND DUBIOUS CLAIMS TO PROMOTE A MEGA-CORPORATE AGENDA ON THE PAGES OF YOUR ILLUSTRIOUS PAPER. WE SAY "YAY!" AND KUDOS TO YOU DEAR SIR FOR RUNNING IT IN YOUR HEALTH AND MEDICAL SECTION. VOILA! OPINION BECOMES TRUTH.
WE'D ALSO LIKE TO THANK YOU FOR NAMING THE ARTICLE 'BREAST ISN'T BEST'. OUR BRETHREN THE FORMULA-PRODUCING MEGA-CORPORATIONS WILL BE TAKING THAT SLOGAN STRAIGHT TO THE BANK. WHO CARES IF IT'S NOT TRUE? TRUTH IS SUBJECTIVE AND PROFIT IS THE ONLY THING THAT MATTERS.
SINCE YOU SO COMPLETELY EMBRACED THE CONCEPT OF PROFIT OVER PEOPLE; WE, THE MEGA-CORPORATIONS, WOULD LIKE TO OFFER UP SOME OTHER POSSIBLE HEADLINES FOR YOUR FUTURE HEALTH AND SCIENCE SECTIONS:
'SMOKING IS GOOD FOR YOU'
'POLLUTED WATER IS DELICIOUS' AND
'EXERCISE IS A WASTE OF TIME'
VIVA LA PROFIT!
The Mega-Corporations

PROFIT OVER INDIVIDUAL RIGHTS, PROFIT OVER DEMOCRATIC PRINCIPLES, PROFIT OVER TRUTH. HECK! PROFIT OVER EVERYTHING!

Being Human

"...And so it is imperative that we embrace the cyborg tendency and utilize a deepening relationship with our technology...." The voice of the invited speaker inserts itself in my psyche. "Uuugh," I mumble to myself and carefully adjust the sling across my shoulder and lean back in my chair, I glance over at my husband. He rolls his eyes, as if to say, "Get a load of this guy." Yeah. Get a load. My fingers begin to jerkily tap my pen loudly on the writing desk in front of me. I look down at your sweet face. "Hi," I find myself saying. Almost startled by your quiet presence and your gaze directly on my face. I smile into your eyes. Hi you. I look back up at 'Mister Embrace the Cyborg' and shuffle my feet. Out of the corner of my eye I see the Head of my Thesis committee doing a discreet wave to get my attention. When I turn toward her, she jerks her head to the speaker. As if to say, "Go get 'em". Yeah. I want a piece of 'Mister I love Technology,' I certainly do, but I point to you and kind of hunch my shoulders. I'm biding my time, waiting for you to fall asleep.

"...As we delve deeper into the genome map, cloning and genetic modification we are moving closer to a super species of..." Oof. Super species? His words hit me like a hammer to the head. Who the hell do these people think they are? I look down at you, just as you start to suck on your hand, eyes rolling sweetly into your head. I know by now that you'll try three times to get milk from your fist. I count. One, as your head falls back and you look around, where's the milk? You descend on your hand again. This time there will be milk! Two, a large suck and you pull away, visibly irritated. Three, you suck intently on your fingers and fist and then your face begins to screw up headed for wail town. Then, I

141

deftly do my own 1,2,3 move. 1. Hand under the shirt, bra unclipped. 2. Shirt pulled up, sling adjusted to cover. 3. Your head brought up with arm for latch on. As your mouth connects, I think about how shy I was about nursing your sister in public. I was always searching for quiet places, out of the way locales to breastfeed in. And here you are, brand new, and we are breastfeeding like professionals. I chuckle to myself. Professional, oh yeah.

   "…Access to these advances will mean that bodily functions will cease to control…." How many times have I breastfed I wonder? I begin to do the math on the notepaper that sits blank in front of me. I breastfeed your sister for 3 and a half years. That's 1,277 days. And you are now 4 weeks old, that's 28 days. 28 days. That's so NEW. I begin to feel the familiar tingling, starting in my shoulders and spreading down the breast, as my milk lets down. A little later than usual, but hey, I'm in a symposium called the Body and Technology; it's a stressful place. I see the little quiver in your chin, as you draw the milk in. Your eyes stare straight ahead at my breast. Memorizing it? That freckle? I heard once that babies develop their eyes better when they have plenty of time to focus on things close up. I'm glad you get these times to rest your eyes from all the clutter of the world. Good for you. Wish I had somewhere to stare besides 'Mister Leave the Body Behind'. What a gasbag.

   "…Already happening in the creation of virtual reality and the commonplace utilization of plastic surgery, the replacement of body has become matter-of-fact…" Hee hee, I think. Yeah, Michael Jackson is matter-of-fact. I look at your sweet little face earnestly feeding, chin quivering working up and down. Your fist curled up, resting beside your mouth, a small bead of sweat just at your hairline. I feel the contentment spread through my body like a deep breath, but deeper. I lean back in my chair, just for a second my eyes glaze. I could sleep, I think. Which I always think right as you fall asleep. Like you have a tether that pulls me in with you. Synchronized. Yep, there it is; your eyes begin to droop, and you're falling asleep. I knew it. I know you. I know your sister too. Although the memories of each breastfeeding eludes me. (How many were there?) I can remember the first, which I wrote poetry about. Exalting. She was perfect too, like you. I remember her skin so pale that the lacework of veins was visible at her temples. I would memorize them when she fed. You, on the other hand, are creamier; your skin seems thicker. Are you stronger, I wonder? You'll need strength to be a baby sister. I hug you closer. And in your sleep you hardly notice.

"...as an expert in the field of human technology, I have seen the exciting studies that show a future when we don't age, never get sick and live forever as information..." I wonder if your sister is having fun at the playground? She's three years old so she has a built-in excuse to miss symposiums. Oh, if only I was three, I would throw some kind of tantrum so that I could go outside and play. But that's faulty logic, because then I wouldn't have you. So, I guess I have to resolve myself to the utter nonsense of the grown up world. Just a few minutes more and you'll be so asleep that I'll be able to ask my question of 'Mister Technophile'.

"...The body has proven unreliable and exceedingly slow, designers are creating implements, which will speed up..." I shake my head to keep these words from settling there, when did slow become so terrible? I start work on my math problem. Okay, I estimate that I have breastfed you and your sister for 1,305 days. Now, how many times a day? I remember the hospital gave me a Guide to Breastfeeding that told me to breastfeed 12 times a day. 12 times. Oh, that seemed like a sufficiently huge amount of time then. Every two hours had to be adequate, right? Then I got your sister home and tried to stick to that schedule. For about a day. She would sleep and sleep sometimes and then nurse every five minutes at others. And at nighttime I would fall asleep holding her in a chair. I realized that schedules were impossible, and then I came to the realization that they are inhuman. Here is that new little baby, flesh of my flesh, blood of my blood, milk of my uh, well food, all trusting and helpless. How could I let this baby cry from hunger? How could I not feed her? I put your sister in my bed and carried her everywhere I went, and never regretted it for a second. And you, oh you were born in my bed. Breastfeeding you was effortless from the start. I have even looked down before and seen you nursing and thought, "When did I pull up my shirt?"

"...The imperfection of our flesh..." How can twelve times a day be adequate for growing such a precious perfect little human? I'm certain that your sister would nurse that many times between 11:30 at night and 3:00 in the morning. She was that kind of girl, and that was when she was 2, she had slowed down. But, maybe I'm exaggerating; I have the habit of doing that. In the interest of science (since I'm in the presence of a scientist who I must say is droning on and on) I'll say that babies breastfeed 12 times a day. 12 times 1,305 equals 15,660. 15,660 breastfeedings. Holy cow, I must be a saint. And you are just a tiny baby; think how many times you'll nurse by the time you wean. Wean. Yikes! Did your eyes just open when I thought that? Are we that in tune? I don't mean to frighten you baby, just put that word out of your head. There's plenty of time in the future for growing up, plenty of time.

"...the body controls too much, we need to find new types of nourishment, input and information that will supercede the outdated..." Every breastfeeding takes at least 25 minutes. But, would I be exaggerating to say that, too? How about 15 minutes, to account for all of the toddler snacks that happened while your sister was standing up and in mid-run. Okay 15 times 15,660 equals 234,900 minutes. Yes. Imagine that. Which is 3,915 hours. And if my math is right is 163 days. Give or take a few. 163 days kicked back with sweet love in my arms, breastfeeding blissfully. Sure I missed out on a bit, 163 days of something else. Something more productive perhaps, more outwardly interesting or compelling. But really, I can't think of anything I'd rather be doing. Nothing. There, you are asleep. I can feel your breaths, deep and regular. I adjust my arm and your mouth slides off my breast, your tongue still slightly moving as if you are still there. Sweet sleep for you. I lean forward in my chair and raise my hand high toward 'Mr. Rejoice in the Super Speedy', who gets a nod from my faculty advisor as if to say yes, pick her question next. Good.

"Mr. Speaker," I say, standing, "How is it possible for you to rhapsodize about a future free of biological restraints, when our most recent experiments in technological replacements have been utter failures?"

"Uh, well, I'm not sure what failure you are speaking of." He replies.

And so I smile and answer, "I'm speaking about the invention of infant formula which was heralded as a miracle replacement for the perfection of breastmilk." I adjust the sling across my shoulder for ease of arm gesturing. " Infant formula, which has lead to the deaths of hundreds of thousands of children worldwide and closer to home, generations of people who are chronically ill…." And so it goes. I speak my mind and suffer his rebuttal, but I think I see him falter, slightly waver. Because it's so true. Breastfeeding is the first food for humans and if we fail so utterly at replacing that, well then, perhaps it's time to resign ourselves to our fetters.

We as babies arrive here so perfect, why can't we embrace ourselves, our lives? Why are we always trying to improve ourselves to our detriment? Infancy must remain this: endless days of feeding and caressing and sleeping and loving and mamas and papas have to devote days and days and days to it. We should understand that by now. Doesn't 'Mr. Improve at Any Cost's' world of speed up and replace seem terribly misguided, as well as frightening? Because it so horribly fails to meet our needs, yet is presented as if it is a change that can't be stopped? I look down at you, your eyes just beginning to open, aware that there are things you need to be awake for. How true. "Watch these guys," I whisper to you, "they'll try to tell you that you aren't perfect, that you'll have to buy perfection. But they're wrong," I promise you. "You are exactly right", I say. You are worth slowing down and being human for.

Heather and Fiona breastfeeding at a Peace March...

Heather Cushman-Dowdee is a one-time wife and three times mother and creator

of Hathor the Cowgoddess, amusing cartoons and insightful/incite-ful commentary about

homebirthing, breastfeeding on demand, maintaining constant contact, sharing space,

unschooling and saving the world. The comics are all completely, truthfully, accurate

portrayals of the life of Heather (as Hathor) except for all the parts she makes up. Which is a

LOT. The usual warnings apply, please do not try this at home (well, of course do the

homebirthing, breastfeeding, slinging, attaching, co-sleeping and unschooling at home,

that's easy and wonderful! Ah heck, you know? There's nothing Hathor does that you can't

do! Go ahead, try!) Heather's work can be seen by visiting her blog at thecowgoddess.com,

and keep coming back please, because the comic changes almost daily (except for when the

Dowdee is family is having some kind of adventure, like traveling, surfing, or camping and

then it's more like weekly...)